A Bridge Between Panic and Peace

30 Days of Inspiration And Scripture

Revd. Bishop Ann Laidlow

Cover design and book editing by
The Write Companion
www.thewritecompanion.co.uk

DEDICATION

*To my wonderful husband,
Steve,
who inspires me and stretches
my thinking
and faith every day.*

www.acorn-int-min.org
www.woftraining.uk

Unless otherwise indicated, all Scripture quotations are
taken from NKJV, ESV, NIV

1st print

Contents

Preface

How to use A Bridge Between Panic and Peace

For the next 30 days, come on a contemplative journey with me as I share some key quotes and scriptures that I have kept close to my heart. Use the MOTIVATE quotes, the MEDITATE scriptures and the CONTEMPLATE pages which are provided for you to write down your thoughts. It's almost like having a journal, a place where you can record all that you hear from God and a way to reflect on what you receive in your quiet time.

I pray for you always to walk in peace.

With love,

Ann

Preface

This little book is an absolute gem! I often discuss with friends the benefits I receive from 'chewing the cud'. If you haven't heard the phrase before, let me explain.

When a cow eats grass, it chews and chews before swallowing, and following this, the cow usually sits in the field, relaxes, and regurgitates the contents of its stomach! I know, sounds a little strange, doesn't it?

However, this is what converts the grass into milk, and so, it is extremely necessary!

I believe that when we meditate on just one scripture throughout our day, when we 'chew the cud', reflecting and meditating on God's Word, we are able to glean so much necessary revelation, thus, God will reveal to us the *value* of meditation.

We can use A Bridge Between Panic and Peace to meditate on a scripture a day, reflecting and contemplating on the wisdom of God's Word. You can start at the beginning or dip in whenever you need the truth and the peace of God.

'I will meditate in thy precepts, and have respect unto thy ways' Psalm 119:15 (KJV)

Revd. Bishop Ann Laidlow has gifted us with some key quotes and scriptures that she has meditated on throughout her years as a pastor, church planter, leader, and mentor. I, for one, and definitely one of many, have gained valuable wisdom from this incredible woman of God. Enjoy!

Revd. Ellie Palma-Cass

~ Your mind is the drawing board of your future ~

~ Meditate ~
'And the Lord answered me: "Write the vision; make it plain on tablets, so he may run who reads it"'
Habakkuk 2:2

~ Motivate ~

**~ When you focus on loving
people rather than reacting
to people your heart grows,
and your energy goes up ~**

~ Meditate ~
*'Let no debt remain outstanding, except the
continuing debt to love one another, for
whoever loves others has fulfilled the law'*
Romans 13:8-10

~ Unforgiveness leaves a door open to the enemy to steal all that is precious to you ~

~ Meditate ~
'Bear with each other and forgive one another if any of you has a grievance against someone. Forgive as the Lord forgave you'
Colossians 3:13

~ Motivate ~

~ Failure is often a temporary condition. It's only when we give up that it becomes a permanent condition ~

~ Meditate ~

'He drew me up from the pit of destruction, out of the miry bog, and set my feet upon a rock, making my steps secure. He put a new song in my mouth, a song of praise to our God. Many will see and fear, and put their trust in the Lord'
Psalm 40:2-3

~ Motivate ~

~ Let your values lead you and don't allow your feelings to push you around ~

~ Meditate ~
'Better is a poor person who walks in integrity than one who is crooked in speech and is a fool'
Proverbs 19:1

~ The path to a miracle is always through uncomfortable terrain ~

~ Meditate ~
'I was pushed hard, so that I was falling, but the Lord helped me'
Psalm 118:13

~ Motivate ~

~ Define the win, before you begin! ~

~ Meditate ~
'They will have no fear of bad news; their hearts are steadfast, trusting in the Lord'
Psalm 112:7

~ Live as if you are who God says you are. Why? Because you ARE who God says you are! ~

~ Meditate ~
'But they are justified freely by His grace through the redemption that is in Christ Jesus'
Romans 3:24

~ Motivate ~

~ You will thrive, if you do not believe the enemy's lies ~

~ Meditate ~
'We demolish arguments and every
pretension that sets itself up against the
knowledge of God, and we take captive every
thought to make it obedient to Christ'
2 Corinthians 10:5

~ You are one word of encouragement away, from making someone else's day! ~

~ Meditate ~
'Therefore, encourage one another and build each other up, just as in fact you are doing'
1 Thessalonians 5:11

~ Motivate ~

~ Sing loud in the middle of a storm! ~

~ Meditate ~
'O my strength, I will sing praises to you, for you, O God, are my fortress, the God who shows me steadfast love'
Psalm 59:17

~ Motivate ~

~ Church is a place where the imperfect meet and plug into the supernatural presence of God, empowered to change their life and their world! ~

~ Meditate ~
'What is the outcome then, brethren? When you assemble, each one has a psalm, has a teaching, has a revelation, has a tongue, has an interpretation. Let all things be done for edification'
1 Corinthians 14:26

~ Motivate ~

~ To rejoice is your choice! ~

~ Meditate ~
'Rejoice always, pray without ceasing, give
thanks in all circumstances; for this is the
will of God in Christ Jesus for you'
1 Thessalonians 5:16-18

~ Motivate ~

~ Don't promise when you're happy,
Don't reply when you're angry,
Don't decide when you're sad
~

~ Meditate ~
'If any of you lacks wisdom, let him ask God,
who gives out generously to all without
reproach, and it will be given him'
James 1:5

~ Motivate ~

~ In order to go from overwhelmed to overjoyed, we must first be overruled by God! ~

~ Meditate ~
'But the Helper, the Holy Spirit, whom the Father will send in my Name, will teach you all things and remind you of everything that I have told you'
John 14:26

~ Motivate ~

~ It is not enough just to be alive. You need to CHOOSE to LIVE! ~

~ Meditate ~
'See, I set before you today life and prosperity, death and destruction. For I command you today to love the Lord, your God, to walk in obedience to Him, and to keep His commands, decrees and laws; then you will live and increase, and the Lord, your God, will bless you in the land you are entering to possess'
Deuteronomy 30:15-20

~ Motivate ~

~ Pack now for where you're planning to be tomorrow, and with the Holy Spirit you can get in all you need! ~

~ Meditate ~

'Go to the ant, O sluggard; consider her ways, and be wise. Without having any chief, officer, or ruler, she prepares her bread in the summer and gathers her food in harvest'
Proverbs 6:6-8

~Motivate ~

~ When we acknowledge our insufficiency and rely on God's power, He can turn our inadequacy into victory! ~

~ Meditate ~

'God stretches the northern sky over empty space and hangs the earth on nothing. He wraps the rain in His thick clouds.. He covers the face of the moon, shrouding it with His clouds. He created the horizon when He separated the waters; He set the boundary between day and night. The foundations of heaven tremble; they shudder at His rebuke. By His power the sea grew calm. By His skill He crushed the great sea monster. His spirit made the heavens beautiful, and His power pierced the gliding serpent. These are just the beginning of all that He does, merely a whisper of His power. Who, then, can comprehend the thunder of His power?'
Job 26:7-14

~ Motivate ~

~ People who spend quality time with Jesus, grow to be more like Him ~

~ Meditate ~
'For those whom He foreknew He also predestined to be conformed to the image of His Son, in order that He might be the firstborn among many brothers'
Romans 8:29

~ Motivate ~

~ The Word of God isn't just to be known, but sown, grown and harvested in our lives to feed the world around us! ~

~ Meditate ~
'You have enlarged the nation and increased their joy; they rejoice before You as people rejoice at the harvest, as warriors rejoice when dividing the plunder'
Isaiah 9:3

~ Motivate ~

~ Life changing is an understatement! The domino effect of your witness will have generational, earth-shattering, eternal, consequences! ~

~ Meditate ~
'With every prayer and petition, pray at all times in the spirit, and to this end be alert, with all perseverance and petitions for all the saints'
Ephesians 6:18

~Motivate ~

~ It's ALWAYS time to pray BIG prayers! ~

~ Meditate ~
'This is the confidence we have in approaching God: that if we ask anything according to His will, He hears us. And if we know that He hears us – whatever we ask – we know that we have what we have asked of Him'
1 John 5:14-15

~ Motivate ~

~ Tomorrow will be different, if you change something today

~

~Meditate ~
'The steadfast love of the Lord never ceases;
His mercies never come to an end; they are
new every morning; great is Your
faithfulness'
Lamentations 3:22-23

~ Motivate ~

~ When God blesses you He has the ripple effect in mind ~

~ Meditate ~

'How abundant are the good things that You have stored up for those who fear You, that You bestow in the sight of all, on those who take refuge in You'
Psalm 31:19

~ Motivate ~

~ God doesn't want to be involved in the plans you have for your life. He wants you to be involved in HIS plans for your life! ~

~ Meditate ~
'I will instruct you and teach you in the way you should go; I will counsel you with My eye upon you'
Psalm 32:8

~ Motivate ~

~ Moving from the familiar to the spectacular means stepping out! ~

~ Meditate ~
'Jesus looked at them intently and said
"Humanly speaking, it is impossible. But
with God everything is possible"'
Matthew 19:26

~ Motivate ~

~ Prayer is the bridge between panic and peace ~

~ Meditate ~
'Peace I leave with you; My peace I give to
you. Not as the world gives do I give to you.
Let not your hearts be troubled, neither let
then be afraid'
John 14:27

~ Motivate ~

~ God takes risks with people, that people don't often take risks with ~

~ Meditate ~
'It is the Lord who goes before you. He will be with you; He will not leave you or forsake you. Do not fear or be dismayed'
Deuteronomy 31:8

~ Motivate ~

~ Your capacity to believe is directly related to your ability to listen ~

~ Meditate ~
'God "will repay each person according to what they have done". To those who by persistence in doing good seek glory, honour and immortality, He will give eternal life. But for those who are self-seeking and who reject the truth and follow evil, there will be wrath and anger'
Romans 2:6-8

~ Motivate ~

~ We, who are nothing, can be filled with Him, Who is everything and that will make us something! ~

~ Meditate ~
'I have filled him with the spirit of wisdom, in understanding, in knowledge, and in all kinds of craftsmanship'
Exodus 31:3

CONTEMPLATE

Note pages for you to write out your thoughts

Printed in Great Britain
by Amazon

61636919R00071